THE ROYAL
HORTICULTURAL
SOCIETY

DIARY
2024

First published in 2023 by Frances Lincoln Publishing,
an imprint of The Quarto Group.
One Triptych Place, London, SE1 9SH
United Kingdom
www.Quarto.com

With thanks to Richard Dee, RHS Horticultural
Taxonomist. Plant names are as they were written at
the time of the original illustrations.

A catalogue record for this book is
available from the British Library.

ISBN 978 0 7112 8288 9

10 9 8 7 6 5 4 3 2 1

Printed in China

Title page *Amaryllis pulverulenta*

Below *Crinum zeylanicum*

RHS FLOWER SHOWS 2024
The Royal Horticultural Society holds a number of
prestigious flower shows throughout the year. At
the time of going to press, show dates for 2024 had
not been confirmed but details can be found on the
website at: rhs.org.uk/shows-events

Every effort is made to ensure calendarial data is
correct at the time of going to press but the publisher
cannot accept any liability for any errors or changes.

CALENDAR 2024

JANUARY
M	T	W	T	F	S	S
1	2	3	4	5	6	7
8	9	10	11	12	13	14
15	16	17	18	19	20	21
22	23	24	25	26	27	28
29	30	31				

FEBRUARY
M	T	W	T	F	S	S
			1	2	3	4
5	6	7	8	9	10	11
12	13	14	15	16	17	18
19	20	21	22	23	24	25
26	27	28	29			

MARCH
M	T	W	T	F	S	S
				1	2	3
4	5	6	7	8	9	10
11	12	13	14	15	16	17
18	19	20	21	22	23	24
25	26	27	28	29	30	31

APRIL
M	T	W	T	F	S	S
1	2	3	4	5	6	7
8	9	10	11	12	13	14
15	16	17	18	19	20	21
22	23	24	25	26	27	28
29	30					

MAY
M	T	W	T	F	S	S
		1	2	3	4	5
6	7	8	9	10	11	12
13	14	15	16	17	18	19
20	21	22	23	24	25	26
27	28	29	30	31		

JUNE
M	T	W	T	F	S	S
					1	2
3	4	5	6	7	8	9
10	11	12	13	14	15	16
17	18	19	20	21	22	23
24	25	26	27	28	29	30

JULY
M	T	W	T	F	S	S
1	2	3	4	5	6	7
8	9	10	11	12	13	14
15	16	17	18	19	20	21
22	23	24	25	26	27	28
29	30	31				

AUGUST
M	T	W	T	F	S	S
			1	2	3	4
5	6	7	8	9	10	11
12	13	14	15	16	17	18
19	20	21	22	23	24	25
26	27	28	29	30	31	

SEPTEMBER
M	T	W	T	F	S	S
						1
2	3	4	5	6	7	8
9	10	11	12	13	14	15
16	17	18	19	20	21	22
23	24	25	26	27	28	29
30						

OCTOBER
M	T	W	T	F	S	S
	1	2	3	4	5	6
7	8	9	10	11	12	13
14	15	16	17	18	19	20
21	22	23	24	25	26	27
28	29	30	31			

NOVEMBER
M	T	W	T	F	S	S
				1	2	3
4	5	6	7	8	9	10
11	12	13	14	15	16	17
18	19	20	21	22	23	24
25	26	27	28	29	30	

DECEMBER
M	T	W	T	F	S	S
						1
2	3	4	5	6	7	8
9	10	11	12	13	14	15
16	17	18	19	20	21	22
23	24	25	26	27	28	29
30	31					

CALENDAR 2025

JANUARY
M	T	W	T	F	S	S
		1	2	3	4	5
6	7	8	9	10	11	12
13	14	15	16	17	18	19
20	21	22	23	24	25	26
27	28	29	30	31		

FEBRUARY
M	T	W	T	F	S	S
					1	2
3	4	5	6	7	8	9
10	11	12	13	14	15	16
17	18	19	20	21	22	23
24	25	26	27	28		

MARCH
M	T	W	T	F	S	S
					1	2
3	4	5	6	7	8	9
10	11	12	13	14	15	16
17	18	19	20	21	22	23
24	25	26	27	28	29	30
31						

APRIL
M	T	W	T	F	S	S
	1	2	3	4	5	6
7	8	9	10	11	12	13
14	15	16	17	18	19	20
21	22	23	24	25	26	27
28	29	30				

MAY
M	T	W	T	F	S	S
			1	2	3	4
5	6	7	8	9	10	11
12	13	14	15	16	17	18
19	20	21	22	23	24	25
26	27	28	29	30	31	

JUNE
M	T	W	T	F	S	S
						1
2	3	4	5	6	7	8
9	10	11	12	13	14	15
16	17	18	19	20	21	22
23	24	25	26	27	28	29
30						

JULY
M	T	W	T	F	S	S
	1	2	3	4	5	6
7	8	9	10	11	12	13
14	15	16	17	18	19	20
21	22	23	24	25	26	27
28	29	30	31			

AUGUST
M	T	W	T	F	S	S
				1	2	3
4	5	6	7	8	9	10
11	12	13	14	15	16	17
18	19	20	21	22	23	24
25	26	27	28	29	30	31

SEPTEMBER
M	T	W	T	F	S	S
1	2	3	4	5	6	7
8	9	10	11	12	13	14
15	16	17	18	19	20	21
22	23	24	25	26	27	28
29	30					

OCTOBER
M	T	W	T	F	S	S
		1	2	3	4	5
6	7	8	9	10	11	12
13	14	15	16	17	18	19
20	21	22	23	24	25	26
27	28	29	30	31		

NOVEMBER
M	T	W	T	F	S	S
					1	2
3	4	5	6	7	8	9
10	11	12	13	14	15	16
17	18	19	20	21	22	23
24	25	26	27	28	29	30

DECEMBER
M	T	W	T	F	S	S
1	2	3	4	5	6	7
8	9	10	11	12	13	14
15	16	17	18	19	20	21
22	23	24	25	26	27	28
29	30	31				

Priscilla Susan Bury (1799–1872)

Within its treasured collections, the RHS Lindley Library holds a copy of *A Selection of Hexandrian Plants* (1831–34) by Priscilla Bury, described as 'one of the most splendid botanical works to be published in England in the nineteenth century'.[1] Images from this sumptuous volume are reproduced here alongside an assortment of Bury's striking creations for *The Botanist* (1836–42) – one of two nineteenth-century botanical journals Bury contributed to during her lifetime. But who was Priscilla Bury and what are hexandrian plants?

Born on 12th January 1799 to Edward Dean Falkner (1750–1825) and Bridgett Tarleton (d.1819), Priscilla Susan Falkner came from affluent beginnings. The family lived at Fairfield, their estate just outside of Liverpool where Priscilla grew up surrounded by extensive gardens and richly stocked glasshouses filled with plants that inspired her budding artistic talents.

Self-taught, she created plant portraits of her favourite forms, becoming a proficient botanical artist. With her skills and portfolio growing, Priscilla was encouraged by her friend William Swainson (1789–1855) to publish her extensive work, with him acting as editor. Unfamiliar with the world of publishing, she approached the botanical writer William Roscoe (1753–1831) for advice, drawing upon his *Monandrian Plants* (1824–28) as a template for her prospective publication. However, after Priscilla's marriage to railway engineer Edward Bury in 1830, her plans altered and she instead independently published *A Selection of Hexandrian Plants* – that is, plants with six stamens.

Issued in parts from 1831 to 1834, the preface describes Bury as an amateur, but her artwork shows

a sensitivity and keen eye for detail. Her original watercolour drawings were based on specimens from the family *Amaryllidaceae* and *Liliaceae*, grown not only at Fairfield, but in Liverpool Botanic Garden and in private collections. These images were reworked for publication by the celebrated engraver Robert Havell (1793–1878) into 51 large aquatint plates, which are not simply visually stunning but provide an intriguing insight into plant breeding in Liverpool in the nineteenth century.[2] The illustrations include the attribution 'Drawn by Mrs. E. Bury, Liverpool' a typical pattern followed in her plates in *The Botanist* and *The Botanic Garden* (1825–51) where she was simply signed 'Mrs E Bury'.

Very few copies of *Hexandrian Plants* were produced, perhaps only enough for the work's 79 subscribers. This included John James Audubon (1785–1851), whose famous publication *The Birds of America*, Havell worked on concurrently. The scarcity of Bury's work makes this rare treasure ever more precious and a privilege to share.

In later life Bury turned from botany to become a scientific illustrator for works on microscopy and would also write a memoir of her husband following his death in 1858. She died at her home in Thornton Heath, also called Fairfield, in 1872.

Jessica Hudson
RHS Rare Books Librarian

1. Lucia Tongiorgi Tomasi, *An Oak Spring Flora* (1997), p. 327.
2. Brent Elliott, *The Cultural Heritage Collections of the RHS Lindley Library* in Occasional Papers from the RHS Lindley Library (2009), p. 39.

JANUARY

01 *Monday*

New Year's Day
Holiday, UK, Republic of Ireland,
USA, Canada, Australia and New Zealand

02 *Tuesday*

Holiday, Scotland and New Zealand

03 *Wednesday*

04 *Thursday*

Last quarter

05 *Friday*

06 *Saturday*

Epiphany

07 *Sunday*

Lilium japonicum

JANUARY

Monday 08

Tuesday 09

Wednesday 10

New moon

Thursday 11

Friday 12

Saturday 13

Sunday 14

Crinum declinatum

JANUARY

---

15 *Monday*   Holiday, USA (Martin Luther King Jnr Day)

---

16 *Tuesday*

---

17 *Wednesday*

---

18 *Thursday*   *First quarter*

---

19 *Friday*

---

20 *Saturday*

---

21 *Sunday*

Amaryllis stilosa

JANUARY

Monday 22

Tuesday 23

Wednesday 24

Full moon

Thursday 25

Holiday, Australia (Australia Day)

Friday 26

Saturday 27

Sunday 28

Amaryllis johnsonii

JANUARY/FEBRUARY

29 *Monday*

30 *Tuesday*

31 *Wednesday*

01 *Thursday*

02 *Friday*   *Last quarter*

03 *Saturday*

04 *Sunday*

Lilium canadense

FEBRUARY

	Monday 05

Holiday, New Zealand (Waitangi Day) Tuesday 06

Wednesday 07

Thursday 08

New moon Friday 09

Chinese New Year Saturday 10

Sunday 11

Crinum cruentum

FEBRUARY

12 *Monday*

13 *Tuesday* — Shrove Tuesday

14 *Wednesday* — Valentine's Day
Ash Wednesday

15 *Thursday*

16 *Friday* — *First quarter*

17 *Saturday*

18 *Sunday*

Lilium superbum, Lilium chalcedonicum, Lilium martagon and white martagon.

FEBRUARY

Holiday, USA (Presidents' Day)

Monday 19

Tuesday 20

Wednesday 21

Thursday 22

Friday 23

Full moon

Saturday 24

Sunday 25

Pancratium amboinense

FEBRUARY/MARCH

26 *Monday*

27 *Tuesday*

28 *Wednesday*

29 *Thursday*

01 *Friday*

St David's Day

02 *Saturday*

03 *Sunday*

Last quarter

Amaryllis longifolia

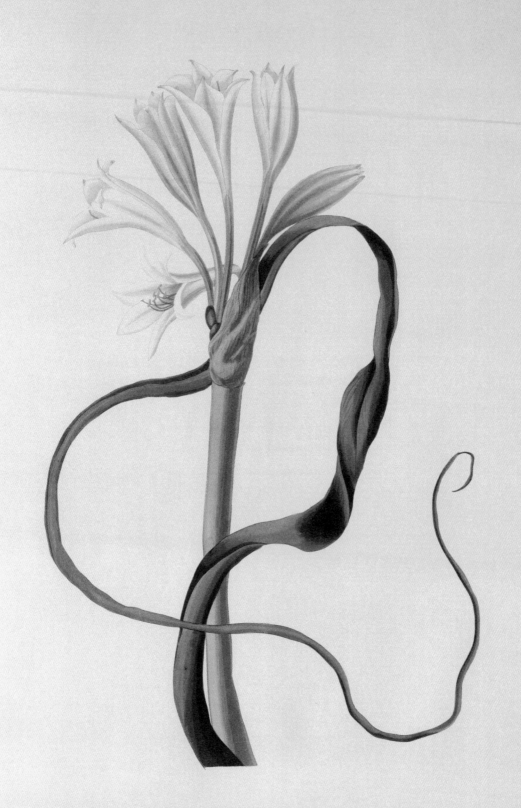

MARCH

Monday 04

Tuesday 05

Wednesday 06

Thursday 07

Friday 08

Saturday 09

New moon
Mothering Sunday, UK and Republic of Ireland

Sunday 10

Amaryllis equestris 'Major'

MARCH

11 *Monday*

Commonwealth Day
First day of Ramadân
(subject to sighting of the moon)

12 *Tuesday*

13 *Wednesday*

14 *Thursday*

15 *Friday*

16 *Saturday*

17 *Sunday*

First quarter
St Patrick's Day

Nerine aurea

MARCH

Holiday, Republic of Ireland and
Northern Ireland (St Patrick's Day)

Monday 18

Tuesday 19

Vernal Equinox (Spring begins)

Wednesday 20

Thursday 21

Friday 22

Saturday 23

Palm Sunday

Sunday 24

Pancratium speciosum

MARCH

25 *Monday*

Full moon

26 *Tuesday*

27 *Wednesday*

28 *Thursday*

Maundy Thursday

29 *Friday*

Good Friday
Holiday, UK, Canada, Australia
and New Zealand

30 *Saturday*

31 *Sunday*

Easter Sunday
British Summer Time begins

Amaryllis solandriflora var.

APRIL

Easter Monday
Holiday, UK (exc. Scotland), Republic of Ireland,
Australia and New Zealand

Monday **01**

Last quarter

Tuesday **02**

Wednesday **03**

Thursday **04**

Friday **05**

Saturday **06**

Sunday **07**

Lilium pyrenaicum

APRIL

08 Monday

New moon

09 Tuesday

Eid al-Fitr (end of Ramadân)
(subject to sighting of the moon)

10 Wednesday

11 Thursday

12 Friday

13 Saturday

14 Sunday

Amaryllis crocata with a butterfly (*Papilio nestor* Brasil)

APRIL

First quarter

Monday 15

Tuesday 16

Wednesday 17

Thursday 18

Friday 19

Saturday 20

Sunday 21

Amaryllis aulica

APRIL

22 Monday

23 Tuesday

Full moon
St George's Day
First day of Passover (Pesach)

24 Wednesday

25 Thursday

Holiday, Australia and New Zealand
(Anzac Day)

26 Friday

27 Saturday

28 Sunday

Delphinium tenuissimum

APRIL/MAY

Monday 29

Tuesday 30

Last quarter

Wednesday 01

Thursday 02

Friday 03

Saturday 04

Sunday 05

Crinum giganteum

MAY

---

06 Monday

Early Spring Bank Holiday, UK
Holiday, Republic of Ireland
Coronation Day

---

07 Tuesday

---

08 Wednesday

New moon

---

09 Thursday

Ascension Day

---

10 Friday

---

11 Saturday

---

12 Sunday

Mother's Day, USA, Canada,
Australia and New Zealand

Satyrium erectum

MAY

Monday 13

Tuesday 14

First quarter

Wednesday 15

Thursday 16

Friday 17

Saturday 18

Whit Sunday

Sunday 19

Amaryllis belladonna

MAY

20 *Monday*   Holiday, Canada (Victoria Day)

21 *Tuesday*

22 *Wednesday*

23 *Thursday*   *Full moon*

24 *Friday*

25 *Saturday*

26 *Sunday*   Trinity Sunday

Amaryllis formosissima

Of all hues, Celestial, Roseate, and gold
And glittering in elegant Splendour, behold
The LILIES, a race to whom Nature has lent
All her Loveliest charms, of Form, Colour, and Scent.
With so many pleasing allurements endued
And by so many light-winged Votaries wooed,
That through all the wide circle of Flora's domain
Where the Loves, & the Graces so constantly reign,
What Tribe can be found so varied, so fair,
Whose forms are so Noble, whose Painting so rare?

MAY/JUNE

Spring Bank Holiday, UK
Holiday, USA (Memorial Day)

Monday 27

Tuesday 28

Wednesday 29

Last quarter
Corpus Christi

Thursday 30

Friday 31

Saturday 01

Sunday 02

Lilium tigrinum

JUNE

---

03 Monday   Holiday, Republic of Ireland

---

04 Tuesday

---

05 Wednesday

---

06 Thursday   New moon

---

07 Friday

---

08 Saturday

---

09 Sunday

Pancratium calathinum

JUNE

Monday 10

Tuesday 11

Feast of Weeks (Shavuot)

Wednesday 12

Thursday 13

First quarter

Friday 14

Saturday 15

Father's Day, UK, Republic of Ireland,
USA and Canada

Sunday 16

Poinsettia pulcherrima

JUNE

---

17 *Monday*

First day of Eid al-Adha
(subject to sighting of the moon)

---

18 *Tuesday*

---

19 *Wednesday*

Holiday, USA (Juneteenth)

---

20 *Thursday*

Summer solstice (Summer begins)

---

21 *Friday*

---

22 *Saturday*

Full moon

---

23 *Sunday*

Amaryllis solandriflora var. or Amaryllis johnsoni

JUNE

Monday 24

Tuesday 25

Wednesday 26

Thursday 27

Last quarter
Holiday, New Zealand (Matariki)

Friday 28

Saturday 29

Sunday 30

Zephyranthes tubispatha and *Zephyranthes candida*

JULY

01 *Monday*   Holiday, Canada (Canada Day)

02 *Tuesday*

03 *Wednesday*

04 *Thursday*   Holiday, USA (Independence Day)

05 *Friday*   *New moon*

06 *Saturday*

07 *Sunday*

Mentzelia stipitata

Islamic New Year

Monday 08

Tuesday 09

Wednesday 10

Thursday 11

Holiday, Northern Ireland (Battle of the Boyne)

Friday 12

First quarter

Saturday 13

Sunday 14

Amaryllis fulgida

JULY

---

15 *Monday*   St Swithin's Day

---

16 *Tuesday*

---

17 *Wednesday*

---

18 *Thursday*

---

19 *Friday*

---

20 *Saturday*

---

21 *Sunday*   *Full moon*

Pancratium amœnum

JULY

Monday 22

Tuesday 23

Wednesday 24

Thursday 25

Friday 26

Saturday 27

Last quarter

Sunday 28

Amaryllis superba

JULY/AUGUST

29 Monday

30 Tuesday

31 Wednesday

01 Thursday

02 Friday

03 Saturday

04 Sunday   New moon

Amaryllis correiensis

AUGUST

Holiday, Scotland and Republic of Ireland

Monday 05

Tuesday 06

Wednesday 07

Thursday 08

Friday 09

Saturday 10

Sunday 11

Echeveria racemosa

AUGUST

12 *Monday*

13 *Tuesday*

14 *Wednesday*

15 *Thursday*

16 *Friday*

17 *Saturday*

18 *Sunday*

Crinum scabrum

AUGUST

Full moon

Monday 19

Tuesday 20

Wednesday 21

Thursday 22

Friday 23

Saturday 24

Sunday 25

Amaryllis striatafolia

AUGUST/SEPTEMBER

26 Monday

Last quarter
Summer Bank Holiday, UK
(exc. Scotland)

27 Tuesday

28 Wednesday

29 Thursday

30 Friday

31 Saturday

01 Sunday

Father's Day, Australia and New Zealand

Amaryllis purpurea

SEPTEMBER

Holiday, USA (Labor Day)
Holiday, Canada (Labour Day)

Monday 02

New moon

Tuesday 03

Wednesday 04

Thursday 05

Friday 06

Saturday 07

Accession of King Charles III

Sunday 08

Lilium longiflorum

SEPTEMBER

09 *Monday*

10 *Tuesday*

11 *Wednesday*   *First quarter*

12 *Thursday*

13 *Friday*

14 *Saturday*

15 *Sunday*

Amaryllis miniata

SEPTEMBER

Monday **16**

Tuesday **17**

Full moon

Wednesday **18**

Thursday **19**

Friday **20**

Saturday **21**

Autumnal Equinox (Autumn begins)

Sunday **22**

Amaryllis psittacina

SEPTEMBER

23 Monday

24 Tuesday

Last quarter

25 Wednesday

26 Thursday

27 Friday

28 Saturday

29 Sunday

Michaelmas Day

Amaryllis reginae

SEPTEMBER/OCTOBER

Monday 30

Tuesday 01

New moon

Wednesday 02

Jewish New Year (Rosh Hashanah)

Thursday 03

Friday 04

Saturday 05

Sunday 06

Crinum erubescens

OCTOBER

07 Monday

08 Tuesday

09 Wednesday

10 Thursday   *First quarter*

11 Friday

12 Saturday   Day of Atonement (Yom Kippur)

13 Sunday

Amaryllis vittata 'Minor'

OCTOBER

Holiday, USA (Columbus Day)
Holiday, Canada (Thanksgiving)

Monday 14

Tuesday 15

Wednesday 16

Full moon
First day of Tabernacles (Succoth)

Thursday 17

Friday 18

Saturday 19

Sunday 20

Crinum pedunculatum with two butterflies (*Papilio antenor* and *Papilio menelaus*)

OCTOBER

21 Monday

22 Tuesday

23 Wednesday

24 Thursday   *Last quarter*

25 Friday

26 Saturday

27 Sunday   British Summer Time ends

Lilium candidum

OCTOBER/NOVEMBER

Holiday, Republic of Ireland
Holiday, New Zealand (Labour Day)

Monday 28

Tuesday 29

Wednesday 30

Halloween

Thursday 31

New moon
All Saints' Day

Friday 01

Saturday 02

Sunday 03

Griffinia hyacinthina

NOVEMBER

04 *Monday*

05 *Tuesday*   Guy Fawkes Night

06 *Wednesday*

07 *Thursday*

08 *Friday*

09 *Saturday*   *First quarter*

10 *Sunday*   Remembrance Sunday

Lophospermum scandens

NOVEMBER

Holiday, USA (Veterans Day)
Holiday, Canada (Remembrance Day)

Monday 11

Tuesday 12

Wednesday 13

Birthday of King Charles III

Thursday 14

Full moon

Friday 15

Saturday 16

Sunday 17

Amaryllis picta

NOVEMBER

18 Monday

19 Tuesday

20 Wednesday

21 Thursday

22 Friday

23 Saturday   *Last quarter*

24 Sunday

Hemerocallis carulea, Hemerocallis japonica, Libellulæ anquis Harris with English Dragon-fly.

NOVEMBER/DECEMBER

Monday 25

Tuesday 26

Wednesday 27

Holiday, USA (Thanksgiving)

Thursday 28

Friday 29

St Andrew's Day

Saturday 30

New moon
First Sunday in Advent

Sunday 01

Crinum hybridum pedunculatum and *Zeylanicum*

DECEMBER

02 *Monday*   Holiday, Scotland (St Andrew's Day)

03 *Tuesday*

04 *Wednesday*

05 *Thursday*

06 *Friday*

07 *Saturday*

08 *Sunday*   *First quarter*

Chloraea longibracteata

DECEMBER

Monday 09

Tuesday 10

Wednesday 11

Thursday 12

Friday 13

Saturday 14

Full moon

Sunday 15

Amaryllis platypetala

DECEMBER

16 *Monday*

17 *Tuesday*

18 *Wednesday*

19 *Thursday*

20 *Friday*

21 *Saturday* — Winter Solstice (Winter begins)

22 *Sunday* — Last quarter

Crinum ornatum

DECEMBER

Monday 23

Christmas Eve

Tuesday 24

Christmas Day
Holiday, UK, Republic of Ireland, USA, Canada, Australia
and New Zealand
Hanukkah begins (at sunset)

Wednesday 25

Boxing Day (St Stephen's Day)
Holiday, UK, Republic of Ireland, USA, Canada,
Australia and New Zealand

Thursday 26

Friday 27

Saturday 28

Sunday 29

Heliconia bicolor

DECEMBER/JANUARY

30 *Monday*   *New moon*

31 *Tuesday*   New Year's Eve

01 *Wednesday*   New Year's Day
Holiday, UK, Republic of Ireland, USA, Canada, Australia
and New Zealand

02 *Thursday*   Holiday, Scotland and New Zealand
Hanukkah ends

03 *Friday*

04 *Saturday*

05 *Sunday*

Coloured *Zephyranthes grandiflora*, entitled *Zephyranthes carinatus* and *Zephyranthes rosea*

YEAR PLANNER

JANUARY	JULY
FEBRUARY	AUGUST
MARCH	SEPTEMBER
APRIL	OCTOBER
MAY	NOVEMBER
JUNE	DECEMBER